SONGS OF THE SAGE

SONGS OF THE SAGE

THE COWBOY POETRY OF

CURLEY FLETCHER

Edited and with a Preface by Hal Cannon

GIBBS SMITH
TO ENRICH AND INSPIRE HUMANKIND

Revised Edition
15 14 13 12 11   5 4 3 2 1

Text © 1986 Gibbs M. Smith, Inc.

Published by
Gibbs Smith
P.O. Box 667
Layton, Utah 84041

1.800.835.4993 orders
www.gibbs-smith.com

Designed by J. Scott Knudsen
Cover designed by Kurt Wahlner
Printed and bound in South Carolina

Gibbs Smith books are printed on either recycled,
100% post-consumer waste, FSC-certified papers or on
paper produced from sustainable PEFC-certified forest/
controlled wood source. Learn more at www.pefc.org.

The Library of Congress has cataloged the earlier edition as follows:

Fletcher, Curley, 1892–1953.
Songs of the sage

Originally published: Los Angeles:
Kellaway-Ide Co., 1931
1. Cowboys—Poetry. 2. West (U.S.)—Poetry. I. Title.
PS3511.L4466S6
1983 811'.52   86-15134
ISBN: 0-87905-257-0 (first edition)

ISBN: 978-1-4236-2064-8 (revised edition)

Contents

Preface

by Hal Cannon

Minnie rarely worried about Curley. How could she? She loved his wild spirit. But as she lay exhausted on that twisted mattress in an old hotel in Cheyenne she suddenly felt uneasy. Her eyes wide open, she had been reliving how she had slowly turned to see the score after a near perfect ride that day at the rodeo. It had been Curley and Minnie's day. He had won bareback, and she took the prize for trick riding. Curley had said, "Luck's with us now." Minnie started from her bed without thinking, threw on a robe, and opened the door.

Down the hall, light spilled from an open room where smoke hung in a ceiling light shade, and from which she could hear the familiar sounds of gambling, drinking cowboys. She moved closer and squinted in. There sat Curley at a table, absorbed in his hand of cards. Under that hand was one last silver dollar which he now tossed to the center.

"Curley," she called.

He looked up, blinked, and said with a throat-dry voice, "we got one more chance, love."

Minnie spun around and marched back into their room and locked the door behind her.

* * * *

CARMEN WILLIAM FLETCHER was born in San Francisco on September 22, 1892. Curley's mother, Benedetta Rossi, had come from Villa Latina, Frosinone, Italy — emigrating first to Canada, then to California. There she met a young English sailor, Harry Fletcher, and they married and started a family. By the time the Fletchers moved to Bishop, California — when Curley was two months old — Benedetta's brothers and father had already successfully accumulated good farm and rangeland on the border of California and Nevada.

Curley would always remember visiting his glamorous older sister, a vaudeville performer in San Francisco, on that day in 1906 when the ground shook and he held on like it was just another wild ride. He was wiry, thirteen, and had curly blond hair. Whether he was riding out the San Francisco earthquake or riding a bucking bronco on the old Fletcher ranch, he did it with total intensity.[1]

Curley Fletcher grew up with an abiding love for his big Italian family and the desert and farmlands of California. He learned horsemanship and the feeling of freedom in the desert from the Paiute cowboys who rounded up wild cows and mustangs in the foothills of the Sierras. Curley was on one of these roundups when word was received that two sisters and a brother had died of mushroom poisoning and that his parents were sick in a hospital. His mother and father survived, but the accident devastated what remained of the family while it also brought them closer together. Curley and his brothers Fred and Harry remained close throughout their lives. And no matter where Curley roamed, his mother always knew where he was.

Cowboys are generally stereotyped, thanks to Hollywood, as exclusively Anglo-American, yet the truth is that this occupation group has always consisted of a varied mix of ethnic backgrounds. The cowboy's work is so charged with cultural elements that it pervades the life of anyone who

10

participates in it. With its own creed, dress, fancy gear, language, poetry, and songs, it often outwardly replaces ethnicity altogether. For many ethnic Americans, being a cowboy represents the ultimate American dream—a new identity on the American frontier. For Curley Fletcher the cowboy life represented freedom. That life took him to hundreds of places, into over a dozen occupations, and through several booms and busts. Bevrely Haller, Curley Fletcher's daughter, remembers her father as a Renaissance man, filled with life, love, and the spirit of adventure, who left a wake of irresponsibility.

In 1914, when Curley and his childhood sweetheart Minna Edna Flesher left for the big rodeo in Cheyenne, Curley was already known for his riding skills in the buckaroo country around his home in Owens Valley. Going to Cheyenne was a gamble for the cowboy and his young wife. When he lost all their winnings and trip money in the poker game that night, he went down to the lobby and did what he did best, creative problem-solving. First he wired home for money, then he sat down, took a pencil out, and on the empty envelope his prize money had come in wrote one of the best-loved poems in the cowboy tradition, "The Strawberry Roan." He couldn't know then that it would become a classic. He didn't know that it would be put to music and become a popular standard in the cowboy repertoire, and he certainly didn't know that he was the first person to take the excitement and sheer kinetic power of a bronc ride and encapsulate it in verse. What he did understand is that he had to do something to charm Minnie after losing all their money. Would he find a place to bunk down that night? Would she ever forgive him?

Throughout his life Curley Fletcher wrote poems and gave them to those he loved. Sometimes they were commemorative gifts, sometimes recompense for his irresponsibility. Curley Fletcher was generous with his poems in the way he was generous with any money he made.

11

By 1917 Curley had gathered quite a few poems together, mostly fantastic stories about cowboys and horses, men and beasts, and that year he and his brother went to Globe, Arizona, to promote and participate in the Gila Valley Stampede. Curley and the younger Fred were inseparable — Curley was the uncontrollable creative spirit, Fred was the salesman — and Fred didn't say a word as he loaded a couple of boxes from a printer in San Francisco into the back of the car. Inside the boxes were five thousand copies of a small red-covered pamphlet, on the cover of which was a photograph of Curley riding a wild bull. The illustration was above the title: *Rhymes of the Round-Up*. Fred had already sold several before Curley saw it. In the booklet were nine poems, all pure cowboy poetry.

Cowboy poetry had been around for some time. This form of folk art was first published in the 1880s when individual poems appeared in ranching trade periodicals. Early in this century folklorists John Lomax and Howard Thorpe traveled to ranches around the Southwest, transcribing memorized recitations and songs from cowboys. By 1910 each had published a collection of cowboy poems.[2] In 1917, when Fred and Curley Fletcher printed their booklet, the demand for good cowboy poems was undeniable. In fact, Curley's poetry was already known in Arizona. He had consented to having "The Strawberry Roan," originally entitled "The Outlaw Broncho," published in the *Arizona Record* in 1915. The editor noted then that the poem had already been published in other "prominent magazines."[3]

Curley was well known in cowboy circles as a good rider and talker. Though he was scarcely 5' 7" tall and weighed only 135 pounds, he was always the center of attention. Cowboys all over the West who knew Curley learned his poems as soon as they came out and then passed them along. The formality of crediting authorship during the amusement of singing and reciting to friends seemed unnecessary as "The Strawberry Roan" strayed far into cattle camps and parlors around the western country. Several people, in fact, take credit for putting the tune to "Strawberry Roan." Once one of Curley's brothers went back to Italy and heard the same tune put to an Italian song. When he asked about the melody he was told that it was an ancient folk song.

Where the simple tune to "The Strawberry Roan" came from was never a concern to Curley Fletcher. He never liked it much as a song, feeling it made a better recitation. It was only when he started hearing it sung over the radio that he decided it was his right to lay claim. His friends, Romaine Loudermilke and Nubbins Patterson, well-known dude ranch performers and members of the Arizona Wranglers, sang it regularly over KNX radio out of Los Angeles. George German in Kansas used it as his signature song on his radio show. And John I. White, radio cowboy singer and cowboy music scholar, sang the song from New York network radio studios as well. Except for those who knew better, the song was considered an anonymous folk song.

By 1925 the song was being performed in the hot cowboy market. In 1931 "The Strawberry Roan" was sung in the New York production of "Green Grow the Lilacs," the popular forerunner of the Broadway musical "Oklahoma." That same year Fletcher went to Hollywood where he met a popular duo, the Happy Chappies, who co-published the song with him, this time with some words changed and with the familiar chorus. With this sheet music published, Fletcher hoped to share in the royalties from his poem. He never did. The song had strayed too far into folk consciousness. Even when Ken Maynard starred in the movie *The Strawberry Roan,* Curley didn't receive significant royalties.

Curley Fletcher was fed up with Hollywood and his struggle to lay claim to his poem. When another cowboy singer, Powder River Jack, claimed the authorship and when Fletcher was not listed as author in a famous folk song collection of 1934, he wrote the editors a letter in which he documented his authorship of the poem in 1914. He concluded his letter, "Any one laying claim to having heard or read 'Strawberry Roan' prior to those dates above mentioned is a damned liar, branded so in the eyes of God, myself, himself, and the devil."[4]

As was true in many of his quests outside the honest work of a cowboy, Curley Fletcher left Hollywood frustrated. He wrote to John I. White, "Hell, I was born and reared here in the West. My earliest memory is of cowmen and cattle. I spent my best years as a cowboy of the old school. I know every water hole, I think, from the Sierra Nevada to Utah. And I still look back to long days and nights in the saddle, at $30 a month, as the happiest of my existence. And I love the desert."[5]

What is it that makes a few words, a melody, a simple design of one individual's creation, so powerful that they can permeate folk conciousness? Curley Fletcher's poems have done this with cowboys, whereas the test of time usually renders most folk creations and their generations of copies and improvements anonymous.

It might be argued that Curley Fletcher's "The Strawberry Roan" became a folk song through the specific circumstances of a supercharged cowboy song market. It is harder to explain Curley's bawdy poems.[6] They are amazing in that they have never been circulated widely in print. They never went to Hollywood, were never performed on the radio, yet for several generations these poems have been passed around and are still widely recited by cowboys today. And unlike "The Strawberry Roan," for which Fletcher received little credit in the world of popular culture, cowboys generally credit these poems to the author. It is regrettable and yet delightful that

14

they are not published here — may they continue to tickle the baser sensibilities of cowboys for another fifty years.

Curley, along with his brothers Fred and Harry, undertook many successful business ventures. For many years they promoted small rodeos around the West, and for a while they published a magazine out of California called *Ride*. Though subscriptions were brisk, an employee pocketed the money and took a ride. Later Fletcher edited yearly collections of stories and poetry, one from Reno called *Silverado* and one from Las Vegas called *Hellderado*. As a cowboy Curley had seen a good deal of back country and had done a fair bit of prospecting. In later years he established a number of mines, several in partnership with Dick Foran and Tex Ritter, and he made a pretty good strike mining tungsten near Darwin, California, during World War II. Though he never appeared in western films, he advised on many scripts and lent his expertise in the areas of stunt riding and cowboy authenticity. He even tried working with Steven Schlesinger Productions on *Red Ryder Comics* in New York City.

In addition to Fletcher's varied careers, he was a musician — not just a cowboy musician but one who played classical music on violin, piano, and guitar — and he was an avid reader who carried the *Rubaiyat* of Omar Khayyam with him religiously. Though he only attended school through the sixth grade, he spoke French and Spanish fluently.

Frank "Shorty" Prunty knew Curley Fletcher in his later years when Fletcher mined near the Prunty ranch outside Elko, Nevada. Curley helped the Pruntys rewire their ranch house and Shorty got a chance to hang around the older Fletcher. Shorty had great admiration for Curley and remembers him as "graceful in his later years." Shorty says, "Curley just talked poetry, just like you and me talking now."[8]

It was to his mine in Nevada that Curley took his young grandson Johnny one day to salt the shafts with minerals. Curley explained to the boy what he was doing. A few days later some mining engineers came to inspect the mine. In the middle of the tour Johnny spoke up, bragging to the engineers that his grandpa had salted the mine just for them. Curley was undaunted, and claimed the salting of the mine was only poetic license.

When Minnie died in 1926, Curley was deeply grieved. Though he was a wild spirit, Minnie had always been there. He remained single for several years, then was married for a short time to the daughter of Guy Welsch, who had illustrated his 1931 book of poems, *Songs of the Sage*. This volume is a replica of that work.

Like S. Omar Barker, Curley Fletcher did not consider himself just a cowboy poet, but a western poet. In this edition we have chosen to feature Curley Fletcher's cowboy poems, yet he wrote in many styles. His formal poems about the West tackle the infinite, the immortal, the universal. These poems, though far different from the raw power of "The Strawberry Roan," are also of Curley Fletcher. The brilliance of all his poetry is in the sounds his words make when read aloud.

Curley Fletcher's last years were spent in Nevada. He was married to Joan Putters from 1945 until his death in 1954. Two funerals were held for him. After a funeral in San Jose, California, where he died, his body was shipped to his home town of Bishop. There his funeral was both a public and a media event. The whole town closed down and "The Strawberry Roan" was played as a dirge during the viewing. Though he probably would have enjoyed the attention, he would have preferred another melody. Perhaps the sermon he would have picked for himself is contained in one of his later poems, "The Tome of Time," where Curley Fletcher questions

16

the significance of his own life in contrast to the immense infinity of the desert and the sky.

Western Folklife Center
Salt Lake City, 1986

1. Bevrely Haller told me these stories of her father during a phone conversation in April, 1986.

2. Howard Thorpe published *Songs of the Cowboys* in 1908, and John Lomax published *Cowboy Songs* in 1910.

3. Curley Fletcher claimed in a letter to John I. White in 1934 that the poem was first published in the *Boulder Creek News*, a California weekly, in 1914.

4. This is excerpted from a letter sent to John A. Lomax after he published *American Ballads and Folksongs* without crediting Fletcher. In subsequent printings, Curley Fletcher was at least credited there as the author along with Lomax's oral source for the song.

5. For a fine complete history of "The Strawberry Roan" and many other cowboy songs, see John I. White's *Git Along Little Doggies*, University of Illinois Press, 1975.

6. In particular, "The Castration of the Strawberry Roan" and "The Open Ledger" are recited by many cowboys all over the West.

7. A reminiscence about Curley Fletcher by Shorty Prunty in May, 1986.

The Tome of Time

I spread my sougans on the windswept plains
Of an arid land, where it seldom rains;
Where the desert ponders in muted mood,
And Death Valley slumbers in solitude.

Far, far to the west a primordial peak,
In primeval beauty, rose bare and bleak,
Over rugged scarps where a primal butte,
In primitive pose, stood stark and mute.

The blistering orb of the setting sun,
Sank down toward the west, and with day near done,
Swift, spiraling whirlwinds swung and swayed,
O'er slopes where shimmering heatwaves played.

I pillowed my head on a pristine stone,
Where countless ages of winds had blown,
And I looked aloft to the azure skies,
Where the swift hawk swoops and the eagle flies.

I pillowed my head and I pondered deep,
Where those restless white sands whisper and creep,
When a susurrus zephyr sighs and soughs
Over drifting dunes and through screwbean boughs.

Taloned and toothed and fanged and thorned,
Destitute, damned, deserted and scorned,
Steeped in eternal starvation, this land,
Seemed wrought by some vengeant, artful hand.

Dregs from the slag of time's melting pot,
This was the waste that Creation forgot;
Primitive, patient, proud, and apart,
Waiting the touch of grim alchemy's art.

And it dawned to me as the sun sank low,
O'er the distant range and the virgin snow,
    That Time was finite — on swift swooping wing,
These arid wastelands an infinite thing.

I saw the saffron sundogs slink,
With stealthy step to the shadowed brink,
    To enwrap the peak in a somber shroud,
With the trailing wisps of a vagrant cloud.

As though they had worsted the sun to route.
In myriad hordes, the stars sprung out,
    And bathed the skies in the eerie light,
The semi-dark of the desert night.

There, in the presence of a stunted sage,
I read an ancient volume — page by page.
    Its characters astral — those orbs on high,
Engraved on a tablet, the farflung sky.

The soft sands whispered in rhythm and rhyme,
That the book I saw was the Tome of Time;
    That it spoke stark truth, nor gave a damn,
For a lost illusion or sordid sham.

How avid I scanned through that ancient scroll,
For glyphs to enmark my immoral soul.
    But no page thereon saw my name engraved,
And reading it so I ranted and raved.

Yet I flattered my soul in my blasphemous dread,
For I feared that those stars might hear what I said.
    And my reason staggered as I stared afar,
At the magnitude of these things that are.

I found that I am infinitely mean,
An atom the stars have perhaps never seen;
    The vain importance of self I had known.
Burst like the bubble an urchin has blown.

Foreword

THIS BOOK is written for the lovers of the great open spaces—the mountains, valleys and deserts that form the Empire of the West.

Its characters are the pioneer, cowboy, teamster (mule skinner), prospector (desert rat), and sheepman (sheepherder).

Most of this work is in the vernacular of these early pioneers of the traditional West. The phrases and idioms are a part of the daily conversations which are still common among these virile, independent, free-hearted, generous men and women who are measured, not by the standard of the accomplishments of their forefathers, but are "sized up" by what they themselves have done. THEY KNOW NO CASTE.

They are the real philosophers of life and their creed is based upon the solid foundation of equality and justice for all. It holds no respect for the weakling, the braggart or the mercenary. They are grateful but leave their gratitude unspoken.

It is characteristic of them to profess an illiteracy and an ignorance of "book learning" which leads the stranger to believe them uninformed upon the many topics of historical fact and natural phenomena.

It would indeed surprise the misinformed individual, were he to hear discussed at the campfire, the "chuckwagon" or the water hole, the myths of the Greeks and Norsemen, the rise and fall of the Roman Empire or the works of Shakespeare.

He would be dumbfounded to find on the table in the "bunk-house," the Rubaiyat of Omar Khayyam, the works of Keats, Voltaire, Dumas, Shaw, Wilde and many others.

Many mining engineers have been astonished at the knowledge of strata and ore which the prospector has at his call. In ordinary conversation he uses odd phrases and lurid descriptive synonyms entirely strange to those outside his realm. His vocabulary seems limited but get him interested in topics of natural formations, strata, ore, or any other geological subject and you will find that he is in a class of his own.

The author was born in the West and has spent his life in that part of it, known as the Great American Desert. He grew to manhood in Inyo and Mono Counties in California and knows the Western States as only a child of the West could know them. He has been cowboy, mule-skinner, prospector and what not, but refuses to admit ever having herded sheep.

While most of this life is now in the background, he still feels the lure of the range and the back-country. The odor of desert sage is still fresh in his nostrils and if he has painted a vivid picture in verse—that is his earnest desire.

THE STRAWBERRY ROAN

I'm a-layin' around, just spendin'
    muh time,
Out of a job an' ain't holdin' a dime,
When a feller steps up, an' sez, "I
    suppose
That you're uh bronk fighter by the
    looks uh yure clothes."

"Yuh figures me right—I'm a good one, I claim,
Do you happen tuh have any bad uns tuh
    tame?
He sez he's got one, uh bad un tuh buck,
An' fur throwin' good riders, he's had lots uh
    luck.

He sez that this pony has never been rode,
That the boys that gets on 'im is bound tuh
    get throwed,
Well, I gets all excited an' asks what he pays,
Tuh ride that old pony uh couple uh days.

He offers uh ten spot. Sez I, "I'm yure man,
Cause the bronk never lived, that I couldn't fan;
The hoss never lived, he never drew breath,
That I couldn't ride till he starved plum tuh
    death.

"I don't like tuh brag, but I got this
    tuh say,
That I ain't been piled fur many uh
    day."
Sez he, "Get yure saddle, I'll give
    yuh uh chance."
So I gets in his buckboard an' drifts
    tuh his ranch.

23

I stays until mornin', an' right after
  chuck,
I steps out tuh see if that outlaw kin
  buck.
Down in the hoss corral, standin'
  alone,
Was this caballo, uh strawberry roan.

His laigs is all spavined an' he's got pigeon
  toes,
Little pig eyes an' uh big Roman nose,
Little pin ears that touch at the tip
An' uh double square iron stamped on his hip.

Yew necked an' old, with uh long lower jaw,
I kin see with one eye, he's uh reg'lar outlaw.
I puts on muh spurs—I'm sure feelin' fine—
Turns up muh hat, an' picks up muh twine.

I throws that loop on 'im, an' well
  I knows then,
That before he gets rode, I'll sure
  earn that ten,
I gets muh blinds on him, an' it sure
  was a fight,
Next comes muh saddle—I screws it
  down tight.

An' then I piles on 'im, an' raises the
  blind,
I'm right in his middle tuh see 'im
  unwind.
Well, he bows his old neck, an' I
  guess he unwound,
Fur he seems tuh quit livin' down on
  the ground.

24

He goes up t'ward the East, an'
comes down t'ward the West,

Tuh stay in his middle. I'm doin'
muh best,

He sure is frog walkin', he heaves uh
big sigh,

He only lacks wings, fur tuh be on
the fly.

He turns his old belly right up to-
ward the sun,

He sure is uh sun-fishin' son-of-uh-
gun,

He is the worst bucker I seen on the
range,

He kin turn on uh nickle an' give yuh
some change.

While he's uh-buckin' he squeals like
uh shoat,

I tell yuh, that pony has sure got
muh goat.

I claim that, no foolin', that bronk
could sure step,

I'm still in muh saddle, uh-buildin'
uh rep.

He hits on all fours, an' suns up his
side,

I don't see how he keeps from shed-
din' his hide.

I loses muh stirrups an' also muh
hat,

I'm grabbin' the leather an' blind as
uh bat.

With uh phenomenal jump, he goes
    up on high,
An' I'm settin' on nothin', way up in
    the sky,
An' then I turns over, I comes back
    tuh earth
An' lights in tuh cussin' the day of
    his birth.

Then I knows that the hosses I ain't
    able tuh ride
Is some of them livin'—they haven't
    all died,
But I bets all muh money they ain't
    no man alive,
Kin stay with that bronk when he
    makes that high dive.

YAVAPAI PETE

Now Yavapai Pete was a cow-
 puncher neat,

From Arizona's fair clime.

Lived in his saddle and punched
 most the cattle

From here to the Mexican line.

His ridin' was sassy, his ropin' was classy,

He liked to mix, mingle, and maul;

Not much of a thinker, was more of a drinker,

And could uphold his end in a brawl.

A face like a hatchet, a head made to
 match it,

And a nose like a pelican's beak;

His legs were all bowed and he was
 pigeon-toed,

With a chin that was plum mild and
 meek.

He'd been in the weather, his skin
 was like leather,

His hands were all horny and rough;

You could see by his stride he was
 just made to ride,

And no broncho for him was too
 tough.

A very good hand with a whole lot of sand,
And a voice like a bellerin' bull.
Pretty much on the brag, and at chewin' the rag
He was a whole corral full.

He once told a tale of hittin' the trail,
A-huntin' new ranges to ride;
They'd hung up a bounty in Yavapai County
For whoever could bring in his hide.

He rode to a ranch and asked if by chance
They needed a good buckeroo.
They said he was rough, but not tough enough,
As a bronk peeler he wouldn't do.

Then he rode o'er a rise and battin' his eyes,
A-lookin' down into a swale,
He'd come to the lair of a she grizzly bear,
And she was a-holdin' the trail.

He took a long strand of barb wire in hand,
And crawlin' along on the ground,
He made a big scoop with that barb wire loop
And they both went around and 'round.

28

Then he mounted that bear with a
  handful of hair,
For a quirt used a live rattlesnake,
He rode with a rush out thru the
  buck-brush,
A-swearin' that beast he would
  break.

To the ranch they did go where Pete hollered
  "whoa,"
Then asked the boss what he'd pay—
"My mount is docile fer I've rode her a mile,
And we're a-huntin' a job today."

The boss called his stack, said. "Come
  to the shack.
You look like you might be alright.
That growlin' old bear, yure ridin'
  right there,
Eat up my old range boss last night."

————— •◦• —————

Old Yavapai Pete he couldn't be beat
At lootin', and shootin', and sin.
The chuck-wagon deck was a sorrowful wreck
When Yavapai Pete butted in.

He fanned his gun fast but they got
  him at last,
And he died with his boots on his
  feet.
The wild West was rid of a danger-
  ous kid
With the passin' of Yavapai Pete.

CHUCK-WAGON BLUES

I wanted to be a wild cowboy;
I wanted to rope and ride;
I wanted to kill wild Indians,
And hang their scalps at my side.

I wanted to eat my meat raw,
And carry my pistols by two's,
And I never thought I would suffer
From having the chuck-wagon blues.

I wanted a gila monster
And a rattlesnake for a pet.
I wanted to eat live scorpions,
And watch the tenderfeet sweat.

I wanted to die with my boots on
Whenever I got the bad news.
I wanted to be a great hero—
Now I'm sick with the chuck-wagon
     blues.

I want to go back to New England;
I am going to make me a change.
I don't like this Western country;
I'm scared of the life on the range.

I don't like their beans or bacon,
And I don't like their mulligan stews.
I don't like their sour-dough bis-
     cuits—
I am sick with the chuck-wagon
     blues.

I'm afraid of a hairy triantula,
And I don't want no bronchos to
   break.
I don't like the howling coyotes;
I am scared of a rattlesnake.

I want to trade these here boots off
For a big pair of brogan shoes.
I am willing to walk if I have to—
I'm sick with the chuck-wagon blues.

I've been bucked off on a cactus,
And a long-horned steer had me
   treed.
I've been walked on by a polecat;
I've been bit by a centipede.

I don't like the grub I get here,
And I don't like no kind of booze.
I don't like no kind of tobacco—
I am sick with the chuck-wagon
   blues.

I want to go back to my daddy,
And I want to see my old maw;
I want to tell my big sister
That I don't want to be no outlaw.

I hate the sight of this country
And I don't like none of its crews.
I don't want to be a wild cowboy—
I am dying with chuck-wagon blues.

31

THE SAGA
OF
BORAX BILL

The day of the long line team is o'er,
The long-line teamster is seen no more,
The cadent notes of the leader's chimes
Are forever buried in bygone times.

———————

Old Borax Bill was a tough old pill,
An old case-hardened sinner
Who went his ways in the early days,
An old time long-line skinner.

He knew more schemes for jerk-line teams,
Than anyone of his time;
He could curse by rote and swear by note,
To music, rhythm and rhyme.

He could drive more span than any man,
And where his leaders are
Is out of sight, where it takes till night
For the wheelers to get that far.

For when to go and where to "whoa,"
A long distance telephone
Was hanging near the leaders ear,
To make Bill's wishes known.

He gave mules hell but he fed them well
And he knew just how to drive;
He could haul more load on a sandy road
Than any man alive.

On his wheeler alone, like a king athrone,
He would tell them what to do
And when he spoke, the hamestrings broke,
Or the chains and stretchers flew.

Old Bill was rough, but he knew his
    stuff
On the up grade of a hill,
And a lazy mule was just a fool
To loaf with Borax Bill.

A hybrid late made coyote bait,
Out on the desert's stones.
The team went on in the early dawn,
As the buzzards picked his bones.

He could make a turn with room to burn,
And never a mule to stand,
And when he'd shout the pointers out,
Their bellies would hit the sand.

His voice would ring up in the swing,
Those mules would hop across
Again and again o'er a tightened chain,
For they knew that he was boss.

He kept some rocks in the jockey-box
To throw at a lazy team;
When he shied a stone a mule would groan
And then Old Bill would scream—

"Get out and hit that collar and bit,
You lazy son-of-a-jack,
I'll be up you, snide, and tan your
hide,
To hang upon the rack."

He'd often say in his blasphemous
way,
That after he had died
He would be no stranger at the
manger,
Where the souls of mules were tied.

And that Borax Smith was just a myth,
With trimmings in between;
He had blown more borax thru his thorax
Than Smith had ever seen.

Now a mule I judge will hold a
grudge
Until his dying day;
An abusive debt he'll not forget,
And with interest he'll repay.

At any rate, one evening late
Old Bill went on the "prod;"
With this in mind he got behind
A mule just newly shod.

With all his might and careful sight
This beast took perfect aim,
In a manner neat with both hind feet
He handed Bill the same.

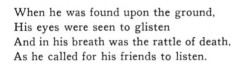

Oh, what a lick was that mighty kick,
And it caught Bill unaware.
With a dismal howl, and a cursing
  growl,
Bill folded up right there.

When he was found upon the ground,
His eyes were seen to glisten
And in his breath was the rattle of death,
As he called for his friends to listen.

From where he lay they heard him say,
"Ain't he a holy terror,
Here I'm busted by a mule I trusted,
Looks like I made an error.

"Now it may be so that it's hot below.
Boys, will you do me a turn,
Just send that fool of a kickin' mule,
Right along with me to burn."

————————•◦————————

Old Borax Bill lies o'er the hill,
Now numbered with the dead
And you may laugh at his epitaph,
For here is what it said.

"Beneath this spot where it's plenty hot,
Lie the bones of a hardened sinner;
Don't be bereft though it's all that's left
Of Borax Bill, mule-skinner."

If he's above or below, I don't know,
Old Bill was kinda sharp,
When they shuffled the deck after the wreck
Bill may have laid hold of a harp.

He knew no school but the hybrid mule,
And he kept them fat and shod;
Old Bill worked hard and he drew a card
That squared his account with God.

———— •• ————

The day of the long line team is o'er,
The long-line teamster is seen no more,
The cadent notes of the leader's chimes
Are forever buried in bygone times.

LONESOME DAYS

The days are lonely for me on the range,
The future seems a void so dark and drear,
You went away and wrought this sudden change,
And I long again your silv'ry laugh to hear.

And always in my memory will abide
The thought of you, that makes my being stir,
As through the lonely distances I ride
A longing for you makes my vision blur.

I listen for your voice again to call
The name I know I never can forget;
The sunshine in my heart — you've taken all
And left me here, alone with stern regret.

I cross the soft green meadow to the
    stream
And watch the sun drop slowly o'er
    the hill;
The wild roses, where I sit and
    dream,
To me are fragrant with your pres-
    ence still.

I hear the good-night warble of a
    thrush
And in the dimness of the fading
    glow,
Peering at me from the underbrush,
I see the outlines of a timid doe.

She is not frightened at my pres-
    ence there,
For now of late she has grown used
    to me;
My loneliness she seems to want to
    share
And her soft eyes seem to shine with
    sympathy.

38

I start back to the linecamp then,
and, hark,

My fancy hears your low, sweet
laugh again;

'Tis but the echoing of the brook at
dark,

Babbling on its way down to the
plain.

And in the evening by the fireside's
glow

My fancy sees your sweet face in the
flame,

Then something seems to choke me,
and I know

For me the range can never be the
same.

Then I seek my lonely bed there by
the lake

And in my dreams forget that you
are gone

Till grim reality bids me awake

To sad, sweet memories of you with
the dawn.

THE COWBOY'S SOLILOQUY

I've ridden afar on the trails of life;
And whether I've been right er wrong
In saddlin' the pleasure, ropin' the
    strife—
I've "follered" the trail right along.

If I ain't got very much knowledge
Of "literchure", "figgers", an' such,
It's because I "growed" up at "cow"
    college,
Where book "larnin" don't count fer
    much.

My youth now is some dim an' distant,
As I'm "jest sorta" on the down grade,
An' old father Time gets insistent
Yet—I don't 'pear to feel much afraid.

Why, if I had my life to live over,
An' was put here to ride this same
    range—
Course I can't say it's "allus" been
    clover—
They ain't very much I would change.

I've played out my hand as I found it;
Busted flushes, an' straits,—All the
    same
I ain't goin' to lay down an' hound it,
Jes' 'cause Time had a seat in the
    Game.

When Gabriel blows his horn for me,
An' I'm tallied along with the dead,
I don't want no cryin' done o'er me
Ner no branded rock put by my head.

Jes' dig me a hole in a hill side,
An' throw in some gravel an' stones;
Cause it might be best on the last ride
If the varmints ain't gnawin' my bones.

I've collected what I had comin',
In the years I've been here on earth.
If I don't get to hear a Harp strummin'
I guess I've got all I was worth.

I've paid fer my drinks as I got 'em,
An' I've toted my end of the load,
Ner I never dealt off of the bottom,
As I scattered my chips 'long the road.

I've never been much of a hedger,
So I'll jes' play the board as it lays;
An' I'll take my chance on Their led-
    ger,
When They round me up with the
    strays.

An' if the devil has got me branded,
When I ride fer the Golden Stair,
An' old Saint Pete leaves me stranded;
They'll be wrong, fer I've allus been
    square.

TIOGA JIM

Now Tioga Jim was a Paiute slim,
The Child of a Forgotten age.
Dirty and sleepy, he lived in a tepee
Near a water hole out in the sage.

A lazy galoot was this greasy Paiute,
Loving the old, old traditions
Bathed in the glory of ancestral story
Of living and dead superstitions.

With an iron shellala he ruled his
  mahala,
As he called on her for his needs.
He'd lay down the law to that whip
  broken squaw
A weaving her baskets and beads.

Silent and grim was old Tioga Jim,
As he smoked in his teepee alone,
Or sipped from a cup in his brush
  wickiup,
And chipped an obsidian stone.

Jim once got his thumb on a bottle of
  rum,
And, feeling that he was in luck,
He lay on his bunk and got "Injun"
  drunk—
A typical old blanket buck.

He went on a war path as an aftermath,
And catching sight of his squaw,
He gave her a lacing, 'twas really dis-
    gracing—
A savage cave man in the raw.

Appeared on the scene with a calm,
    sedate mien,
A souvenir-seeking old patron,
Who opened her eyes in a wild sur-
    prise—
A shocked old society matron.

She burst from her languor in a justi-
    fied anger.
And with an all ireful screech
She wended her way to the midst of the
    fray,
Then broke into clamorous speech.

The buck remained mute as she termed
    him a brute,
A beast and a low filthy hog,
An ignorant savage, the carion ravage
In the paunch of a yellow cur dog.

She said without fail she would have
    him in jail,
And hung by the neck until dead.
Old Jim stood close by with a cold,
    baleful eye,
Then turned to the matron and said:

Pardon me please. You appear ill at
    ease;
I'm sorry I seem to be rude.
Your chivalrous intent is no doubt well
    meant;
However, I fear you intrude.

Recalling a knowledge gained at Car-
    lysle College,
Of which I'm a post-graduate,
In the home of a peer we must not
    interfere.
Your meddling I can't tolerate.

Your militant manners, your falsified
    banners,
Your command of the vile epithet
Arouses my ire and, I fear, may trans-
    pire
In permitting myself to forget.

My relation to, and the courtesy due
Your sordid, haughty veneer,
Which likes not the flavor of my bestial
    behavior;
Excuse me—at least I'm sincere.

Were I to chastise you, 'twould surely
    surprise you
And give me great satisfaction.
Ere you get in the whorl of a domestic
    quarrel,
Beware the potential reaction.

Our destiny lays over divergent ways.
And as to my squaw—well, indeed
She takes no recourse in a court of
    divorce—
'Tis beyond the ken of her creed.

The blood in our veins is pure as the
    rains—
Has been so for numberless ages—
While your hybrid white man is a poly-
    glot clan,
Derived of long virtueless stages.

But a contamination your civilization,
Your alcohol, drug and disease.
There is no excuse for your vile abuse;
Remove yourself, if you please.

THE SHEEP-HERDERS LAMENT

I have summered in the tropics,
With the yellow fever chill;
I have been down with the scurvy;
I've had every ache and ill.

I have wintered in the Arctic,
Frost-bitten to the bone;
I've been in a Chinese dungeon,
Where I spent a year alone.

I've been shanghaied on a whaler;
And was stranded on the deep,
But I never knew what misery was,
Till I started herding sheep.

The camp boss now is two weeks
   late,
The burro dead three days.
The dogs are all sore footed, but
The sheep have got to graze.

They won't bed down till after dark,
And they're off before the dawn;
With their baaing and their blatting
They are scattered and they're gone.

I smell their wooly stink all day
And I hear them in my sleep;
Oh, I never knew what misery was,
Till I started herding sheep.

My feet are sore, my boots worn out;
I'm afraid I'll never mend;
I've got to where a horny-toad
Looks like a long lost friend.

The Spanish Inquisition might
Have been a whole lot worse,
If instead of crucifixion, they
Had had some sheep to nurse.

Old Job had lots of patience, but
He got off pretty cheap—
He never knew what misery was,
For he never herded sheep.

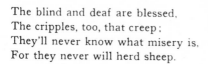

It's nice enough to tell the kids,
Of the big old horny ram,
The gentle soft-eyed mother ewe,
And the wooly little lamb.

It's nice to have your mutton chops,
And your woolen clothes to wear,
But you never stop to give a thought
To the man that put them there.

The blind and deaf are blessed,
The cripples, too, that creep;
They'll never know what misery is,
For they never will herd sheep.

THE POT WRASSLER

How are you there cowboy, I hope you
    are well,
Jest light from your saddle and rest fer
    a spell.
Here are the makins', so roll you a
    smoke,
Yure jest out uh town and I bet you
    are broke.

Yuh looks like old hunger was a ridin'
    yuh hard,
So sit down and eat—you are welcome
    old pard.
I put a lot uh years at a ridin' the range,
But now I am wrasslin' pots fer a
    change.

Now I ain't no chef like that Del-mon-
    a-co,
But I sabes the mixin' of old sour
    dough.
I sorts all the big rocks out uh the
    beans,
And I don't wipe the fryin pans off on
    my jeans.

Muh chuck is all right, and the wagon
    kept neat;
If yuh don't like the cookin', yuh don't
    haf tuh eat.
Oh, I'm a pot wrassler, but I ain't no
    dub,
Fer I'm close to my bed, and I'm close
    to the grub.

I'm a leetle bit old, and I don't want no
truck
With horn hookin' cattle, ner horses
thet buck.
I've rode a long time and my laigs is
all bowed;
I've got to the age thet I'm easily
throwed.

I got the rheumatics and my hands is
all burned,
My joints is all stiff and my belly's all
churned.
Now I'm a pot wrassler, yure a-hearin'
me shout.
So come on and get it, 'fore I throws it
out.

You fellers rope steers to down 'em
and tie 'em.
Then I comes along to skin 'em and
fry 'em.
I got forty a month, and the cookin' to
do,
So I'm all through bein' a cow buck-
eroo.

When you punchers is out in the bliz
zard an' storm.
I'm close to the fire, where I keeps my
self warm.
So do yure old ridin', you wild galoots,
And I'll wrassle pots, you can just bet
yure boots.

WHEN DESERT FLOWERS BLOOM

Tonight, in this big busy city,
So far from the home I have known,
I am filled with a sadness and long-
   ing—
Mid thousands I am lost and alone.

I am pining for my old desert home-
   stead,
Where the moon and the stars shine
   so bright;
To again smell the sage and the
   greasewood,
While the coyotes howl through the
   night.

When the flowers of the desert are blooming,
And the swallow is building its nest
Where the high guardian peaks are a-looming
O'er my old desert home in the west.

There soon again I'll be drifting
When the hummingbird takes to the
   wing,
Where the restless sands are
   a-shifting,
When the desert flowers bloom in
   the spring.

I long for the creak of a saddle,
And I yearn for the touch of the
  reins;
I pine for the buzzing sidewinder,
And the free running blood in my
  veins.

I listen for the call of the eagle,
And the music of the myriad things;
I crave for a drink of the water
That flows from the alkaline springs.

I miss the blessings and the hardships,
The freedom of the wild desert lands;
And I miss the mirage that pictures
A beautiful lake on its sands.

I am going back to the homestead,
I am counting the days, every one;
Till again I can gaze in the distance
At an amber and gold setting sun.

THE PAINTED TRAIL

Oh, Master, I've followed the Painted
   Trail
These many years that have gone;
I have followed the lure of the gold-
   en gleam,
Which ever has led me on.

Thru the Valley called Death, with
   its heat of hell,
O'er the rimrock, granite and shale,
Where the bones of the tortured
   gleam in the sun,
I have followed the Painted Trail.

With a yearning to grasp unlimited
   wealth,
Her secrets I strove to steal;
She clutched them close to her vam-
   pire breast
And hid them beneath her seal.

I have spent my life on these withering sands,
Where the hills lie bleak and bare,
Where hope leads on tho the dry lips parch
Under the sun's mad glare.

The mirage tempts the thirst-crazed
  on
To a fancied lake in a swale,
And they stagger and fall on an
  arid waste;
'Tis their end of the Painted Trail.

From the Funeral Range to the Rio
  Grande
I have suffered the terrible thirst
That oft grips a man in this wreck-
  age of hell—
Oh, God, how often I've cursed.

The years I have spent in this great alone,
The tortures I've suffered untold—
All have passed to the great beyond
And I'm tired, and bent, and old.

Tired of the lust which drove me on,
The hunger, the hardship, the pain,
That drive men mad in this great
  out-doors
With their greedy lust for gain.

I have placed life's greatest bet and lost
Far from the Great White Way,
The wheel of fortune coppers the bet
And the carrion wait for their prey.

The satanic bursts on me now,
And I'll suffer a horrible death.
Soon I will rant, and froth, and fume,
To curse with my dying breath.

I have neared the end of the Painted
Trail
And for me it ceases to glow;
Its hue has changed to a hideous
gray
And it sneers at my tale of woe.

Soon I will pass o'er the Great Divide,
For I hear Thy welcome hail;
Oh, Master, guide and forgive me all
At the end of the Painted Trail.

—————— •• ——————

The sun sinks low in an amber glow,
As a buzzard wheels o'er head,
And the rising sun shone on the
skeleton bone
Of the desert's last toll from the
dead.

THE COWBOY'S PRAYER

Out on the Western prairies,
While riding after stock,
A cowboy met a shepherd
A-tending to his flock.

The herder asked the cowboy
If he would like to stay,
To join him in a little drink
And put some grub away.

The cowboy said, "That's good enough.
When my belly's full of stew,
We'll bury the old tomahawk
And have a drink or two."

The herder cooked up quite a feed
And the cowboy ate his share.
The herder got the jug out
And they started in from there.

The cowboy said, "Let's have a drink,
We'll forget about our war.
Well, sure, let's have another one
And then we'll have one more."

"Your liquor's good," the cowboy
     said
"It surely hits the spot."
"Help yourself," the herder says,
"And we'll have another shot."

Back and forth they passed the jug,
Until they went to sleep;
This puncher of the cattle
And this herder of the sheep.

The cowboy slept beneath a sage
And he was awful tight;
He rolled and tumbled all about
And snored with all his might.

His arm fell o'er a triantula's hole
Which made the spider mad;
He sank his fangs into the arm
And gave it all he had.

The cowboy waked and sobered up,
His arm was swelled and black.
He awakened the sheepherder
And they started for the shack.

The herder said, "That's pretty bad,
Looks like your judgment day.
If I was in your boots, cowboy,
I'd start right in to pray."

"I'd like to pray," the cowboy said,
"But I don't know just how;
I'm goin' to do the best I can,
And I'd better start right now."

So he braced himself upon his knees
And raising up his head,
He cast his eyes toward Heaven,
And this is what he said:

"Oh, God, if You see this poor cow-
    boy,
Come down and lend him a hand.
Don't send Your Little Son, Jesus,
Boys sometimes don't understand.

"Oh, God, I'm not one of them
    sinners
That's callin' You right along,
I wouldn't take Your time up,
Unless there's something real wrong.

"I'm a damned good bronk buster
And a ropin' son-of-a-gun;
It's many an outlaw I've ridden,
And it's many a dollar I've won.

"I've always been good to my horses,
Till today, I never ate sheep.
I never did shirk on no roundup,
And I've always been worth my keep.

"I never have rustled no cattle,
I ain't never took up with no squaw
I ain't never fought 'less I had to,
Then I never went first for the draw.

"Of course, You know better than I do,
But it don't seem to be hardly right
For me to be cashin' my chips in
From a pot-bellied spider's bite.

"He crawled up while I was sleepin'
And he bit me while I was drunk;
I don't want to be belly-achin',
But that was the trick of a skunk.

57

"If I was hurt ridin' a broncho,
Or ropin' a steer, don't You see,
I wouldn't be here a beefin',
I'd figger it was comin' to me.

I've lived by my creed as I saw it,
And all that I ask is what's fair;
If You have been keepin' the cases
You know that I've been on the
    square.

"I never was strong for sky-pilots,
There's no place on them for to lean;
'Cause they ain't much better than I am,
I guess You know what I mean.

I'm usin' a lot of Your time, I guess,
'Cause I don't know just how to pray,
But I won't ask any more favors
If You find time to help me today."

———— •• ————

This was the prayer of the cowboy,
A prayer that was frank and sincere,
When he called on his God as he saw Him,
To lend him a listening ear.

And the cowboy's God must have
    heard him
Out on the plains that day,
For He healed the suffering rider
And sent him upon his way.

THE RIDGE-RUNNING ROAN

It was up in the Bad Lands, I was rangin' alone,
I first heard of this cayuse, The Ridge Runnin' Roan.
He was fleet as a deer and as tough as a mule,
Pretty as a picture and nobody's fool.

High headed and leggy, he was just built for speed;
The cowboy that roped him could own that there steed.
I figured the reason this bronk was still free
Was he never had crossed a mustanger like me.

So I went right to work and I got me a pair
Of the best saddle horses that ever wore hair.
I hunted that mustang and I took to his trail;
When he hit for the ridges he was packin' the mail.

I never did head him nor turn him about,
I aimed to just trail him till I wore him plum out.
Then for five or six days I gained not an inch;
He was wearin' no crutches and that was a cinch.

59

He was tough as a boot and as wise
    as a fox;
He kept on the ridges and a-dodgin'
    the rocks.
I'd trail him till dark and at dawn
    I'd begin,
Till I got pretty weak and my horses
    got thin.

    I followed those tracks till I got stiff and sore,
    But he stayed right in front where he kept makin' more.
    Then I got so I felt like a tired, locoed sheep,
    A-trailin' that fuzztail and a-losin' my sleep.

He went short for water, with no
    time to graze,
While I camped on his trail for
    seventeen days.
Then he got awful gaunt — he was
    wearin' out fast,
Till he looked like a ridge runnin'
    ghost at the last.

    He was placin' his feet like he's walkin on tacks,
    Till I saw he was leavin' fresh blood in his tracks.
    So I started to crowd him and turned him around,
    He quit the rough ridges and hunted soft ground.

I shook out a loop when we got to
    a flat,
I threw that riata and it fit like my
    hat.
He sure gave up quick when I jerked
    out the slack,
Then I noticed some old saddle
    marks on his back.

I had done myself proud and I felt
like a champ

When I got him all haltered and
headed for camp.

He was strikin', and kickin', and
plum fightin' mad.

I could see he was spoiled and sure
enough bad.

Well, I got him at home and into the corral,

I fed him some hay and some oats for a spell.

When he got fat and strong I gave him the news,

I hog-tied him down and nailed on some shoes.

Then I put on the bridle and I fixed
it to fit,

It wasn't the first time that he'd
champed a bit.

I threw on my saddle and I cinched
it right down.

Then I crawled his old carcass—I
was headed for town.

I drug out my quirt, 'cause to me he looked tame,

Like a twenty-two pistol on a forty-five frame.

I got a deep seat and I froze to the cantle,

I jabbed in my meat-hooks clear up to the handle.

He let out a bawl and he went from
that spot

Like the ground where he stood had
sudden got hot.

He topped that first jump with a
shimmy and shake,

Like a-poppin' the head from a live
rattlesnake.

Then he went to sun-fishin', he sure
    was a peach,

And I turned from a wild-cat into a
    leech.

He was mad as a hornet and I guess
    he saw red,

He was handy afoot and his feet
    wasn't lead.

I thought I was up on the hurricane deck

Of an earthquake and a cyclone a-havin' a wreck.

I was doin' my best and was just gettin' by,

But he's doin' better with blood in his eye.

He was duckin', and dodgin', and a-
    walkin' the dog,

He had me so dizzy I was lost in
    the fog.

And then he got busy and the things
    that he did

Was like a volcano that had blew off
    the lid.

He was bawlin', and gruntin', a-
    humpin' the hump;

He turned wrong side out with
    every new jump.

At ridin' bad horses I'm no crippled
    squaw,

But he showed some tricks that I
    never had saw.

With a giratin' jump he goes over
  the gate,

And I grabbed for the horn, but I
  was too late.

He hit with a jar that 'most shed his
  hair;

It busted me loose and I quit him
  right there.

Of all the bad horses that I ever rode,
None was like him, for he seemed to explode.
He busted me up and I'm still stiff and lamed—
That Ridge Runnin' Outlaw will never be tamed.

The last time I saw him, he was crossin' a bridge,
He was high-tailin' back to his favorite ridge.
I've borrowed an outfit as I've none of my own—
My riggin' ran off on the Ridge Runnin' Roan.

THE SADDLE TRAMP

They call me Scum, the saddle bum.
Ever since the day
I quit the strife of a cowboy's life,
To travel, sing and play.
A saddle tramp from ranch to camp,
Just riding near and far;
A horseback bum to sing and strum
On a Mexican guitar.

I used to work, but now I shirk,
And never more will hire
To mark an ear, to turn a steer,
Nor tend a branding fire.
The pie and cake is mine to take—
The best of everything—
I may lay my head on the softest bed,
If I'll blow my harp and sing.

Oh, here or there or anywhere
That I may choose to roam,
Me they'll feed and my saddle steed
Will always find a home.
I'll tell you that my horse is fat.
And I want you to know
It's mighty fine to ride grub line,
And I'm welcome where I go.

I stay a while to sing and smile,
But when there comes a rift
And things get cool, I ain't no fool,
I fork my bronc and drift.
I ramble down to a little town,
As winter comes along,
To little Neta, my Senorita,
And sing for her my song.

When white snow flies from wintry
    skies
And mantles hill and plain,
I'm coming back to that little shack,
And love you dear, again.
My Spanish Neta, sweet Senorita,
Again I've come to you.
So don't you grieve until I leave—
While here I will be true.

THE DESERT RAT

Ah, these tales of the desert's trails!
How oft' they have been told,
By the men who grope in a forlorn
 hope
For the desert's hidden gold.

———— •• ————

I'm off of a hike where I made a
 strike,
Out to the Painted Butte;
I'm a-gettin' old but I know my gold,
And that's a real ore chute.

I've follered the pack on a burro's back
Fer more than fifty year';
But you jest bet I'm a good man yet,
So be it, I still be here.

Jest stake your hat, I'm a desert rat,
And I sabes a burro's wiles;
I ought to know, I guess it's so,
I've trailed 'em a million miles.

I've studied ore and what is more
I'm bound to strike it rich.
The desert's tried to tan my hide,
But I know her every itch.

I've tried to make a loafin' stake
Since Brigham Young came West;
It's the first I've struck of any luck,
Be it so, I've did my best.

By occupation I know formation,
And you can bet yure shirt,
I know the gist of sand and schist
Or any kind uh dirt.

I want to state, I know the slate,
The birds-eye porphry, too;
The bluish-green of serpentine
Fer me ain't nothin' new.

The diorite, the hard quartzite,
The granite, and the shale;
The andacite, and the rhyolite—
On these I never fail.

The azurite in the argentite,
And the flaming travertine;
The sylvanite, and the tremolite
Are ores I've often seen.

The potash salts in nature's vaults,
And all the boric clan;
The colemanite and the pandermite,
I've seen 'em boy and man.

I've pillowed my head on a nitrate
  bed,
I know the very worth
Of hard sulphides and soft chlorides,
Or most the ore on earth.

Now be it so, that I want to go
Back to that Painted Butte;
Right where I found, in virgin
  ground
A genuine ore chute.

I'd like to bet I strike it yet,
And if I don't, I'm a liar.
I'll put my stamp on a new gold
  camp
That will set the world afire.

The mills will grind the ores I find,
And o'er the new town site,
On a concrete road to my mammoth
  lode
A city will spring o'er night.

Now here's the rub, I've got no grub,
No dust left in my poke;
I've got to make a new grub-stake,
In fact, I'm stony broke.

But here's a way to make it pay,
I'll leave it up to you
To lend a hand with the bacon and,
Then we'll cut the claim in two.

I'll go you cow if you stake me
    now
To the little that I'll eat—
Some flour and beans, a pair of
    jeans,
Some boots to shoe my feet.

Well, thank you pard, I know it's hard,
But wait till I return;
You won't regret the day we met,
We'll both have gold to burn.

———————— •• ————————

Ah, these tales of the desert trails!
How oft they have been told,
By the men who grope in a forlorn hope
For the desert's hidden gold.

On their patient feet in the torrid heat,
How many fell between
The water holes, when they freed their souls,
Where their bones were never seen.

THE COW PONY'S LAMENT

I've been on my last big round-up,
I have finished the long days' work,
For the many men who have rode me,
Who know that I did not shirk.

I was ridden by many masters,
Kind, considerate, and true;
Mastered by many riders
Who whipped and cursed me thru.

I, once the pride of the round-up—
Proud, and agile, and sleek,
Have served my time and I'm tired,
And blemished, and old, and weak.

This spring not of the remuda,
I'm aged and useless to stride;
Weathered, and worn, and weary,
By many the long day's ride.

Oft was I proud of the burden
Of a man I could understand;
Whose spurs were only a habit,
He of the soft voice and hand.

To him I gave my best efforts,
To him I loaned my great speed;
And 'twas he who loosed the cinches
As he recognized my need.

But the parasite of the outlands—
The whipping, spurring fool,
The drunken, cursing demon,
The child of a devil school—

'Twas he who has aged me early—
Because of him am I done;
A worn and worthless old cayuse
Going out with the setting sun.

Caught in the last great round-up
That hasn't the dust and the din,
Joining the endless trail herd
As the Big Boss gathers His in.

THE FLYIN' OUTLAW

Come gather 'round me, cowboys,
And listen to me clost
Whilst I tells yuh 'bout a mustang
That must uh been a ghost.

Yuh mighta heard of a cayuse
Uh the days they called 'em a steed
Thet spent his time with the eagles
And only come down fer his feed.

He goes by the name of Pegasus,
He has himself wings to fly;
He eats and drinks in the Bad Lands,
And ranges around in the sky.

Seems he belongs to an outfit,
Some sisters, The Muses, they say,
And they always kep 'im in hobbles
Till he busts 'em and gets away.

Fer years they tries hard to ketch 'im,
But he keeps right on runnin' free;
The riders wore way too much
    clothes then,
Cowboys was knights then, yuh see.

72

He sure bears a bad reputation,
I don't sabe how it begin,
Part eagle, part horse, and a devil;
They claims that he's meaner than sin.

I'm a-ridin that rimrock country
Up there around Wild Horse Springs,
And I like to fell out uh my saddle
When that bronk sails in on his wings.

I feels like I must be plumb crazy,
As I gazes up over a bank,
A-watchin' that albino mustang
Uh preenin' his wings as he drank.

Finally he fills up with water,
Wings folded, he starts in to graze,
And I notice he's headin' up my way
Where I straddle my horse in a daze.

And then I comes to, all excited,
My hands is a-tremblin' in hope,
As I reaches down on my saddle
And fumbles a noose in my rope.

Ready, I rides right out at him
Spurrin' and swingin' my loop
Before he can turn and get goin'
I throws—and it fits like a hoop.

I jerks out the slack and I dallies,
I turn and my horse throws him neat,
And he lets out a blood curdlin' beller
While I'm at him hogtyin' his feet.

I puts my hackamore on him,
And a pair uh blinds on his eyes;
I hobbles his wings tight together
So he can't go back to the skies.

I lets him up when he's saddled,
My cinch is sunk deep in his hide;
I takes the slack out uh my spur
   straps
'Cause it looks like a pretty tough
   ride.

I crawls him just like he was gentle,
I'm a little bit nervous you bet;
I feels pretty sure I can ride 'im,
I still has his wings hobbled yet.

I raises the blinds and he's snortin',
Then moves like he's walkin' on eggs;
He grunts and explodes like a pistol;
I see he's at home on his legs.

Wolves, and panthers, and grizzlies,
Centipedes, triantlers, and such;
Scorpins, snakes, and bad whiskey
Compared to him wasn't much.

I got a deep seat in my saddle
And my spurs both bogged in the cinch;
I don't aim to take any chances,
I won't let him budge me an inch.

He acts like he's plumb full uh loco,
Just ain't got a lick uh sense;
He's weavin' and buckin' so crooked
That I thinks of an Arkansaw fence.

I'm ridin' my best and I'm busy
And troubled a-keepin' my seat;
He didn't need wings fer flyin',
He's handy enough on his feet.

He's got me half blind and I weaken
He's buckin' around in big rings;
Besides which he kep me a-guessin',
A-duckin', and dodgin' his wings.

By golly he starts gettin' rougher,
He's spinnin' and sunfishin', too,
I grabs me both hands full uh leather;
I'm weary and wishin' he's through.

He hits on the ground with a twister
That broke the wing hobbles,
  right there;
Before I can let loose and quit him,
We're sailin' away in the air.

He smoothes out and keeps on a
  climbin'
Till away down, miles below,
I gets me a look at the mountains
And the peaks all covered with snow.

Up through the clouds, I'm a-freezin',
Plumb scared and I'm dizzy to boot;
I sure was a-wishin' I had me
That thing called a paramachute.

And then I musta gone loco,
Or maybe I goes sound asleep,
'Cause when I wakes up I'm a-layin'
Right down on the ground in a heap

He may uh had wings like an angel
And he may uh been light on his feet,
But he oughta had horns like the devil
And a mouth fit fer eatin' raw meat.

I've lost a good saddle and bridle,
My rope and some other good things,
But I'm sure glad to be here to tell
    yuh
To stay off uh horses with wings.

MOUNTAIN MEADOW
MEMORIES

As the grouse drum in the pine,
As the silvery moonbeams shine;
Those happy days I live again
In memory's pathos, memory's pain.

All is lost to me but these
Mountain meadow memories;
Of the days we used to ride
Thru the meadows side by side.

All my laughter, all my tears,
Buried deep in yesteryears;
Thoughts of you that haunt me still
Thru summer's sunshine, winter's
     chill.

My fancy pictures you once more,
Waiting near the cabin door;
Yet, all is lost to me but these
Mountain meadow memories.

Memories of high mountain meadows
Beneath peaks of perpetual snow;
Memories of days in their shadows,
With you in the long, long ago.

Memories recalling the echos
Of the babbling brook on its way
Down to the plain where I met you—
Living memories of dead yesterday.

LAST OF THE THUNDERING HERD

There in that limited pasture,
Their eyes bedimmed and blurred;
Standing like captives in prison,
The last of the thundering herd.

Of the numbers once dotting the
    prairie
Are these all that remain?
Has the echo of numberless, patter-
    ing feet
Forever a-gone from the plain?

Of the countless thousands that
    herded
In answer to nature's call,
Migrating north in the springtime,
Wandering south in the fall.

Crossing the snow-covered moun-
    tains,
Leaping their treacherous seams,
Spanning the riotous rivers,
Fording tumultous streams.

Roaming at will o'er the prairies,
Care-free and seeking no goal;
A few to fall by the wayside,
The wolf, or the Indian's toll.

Came then the white man westward,
To the land of the bison's birth;
Begruding an unharrassed moment,
Annihilating them from the earth.

Madly and tirelessly hunted,
Ruthlessly, wantonly slain;
Their carcasses dotting the prairies,
Their stench permeating the plain.

And there are the last of the bison.
Ah! but it seems so absurd—
The black page of our civilization,
The last of the thundering herd!

WILD BUCKEROO

I been ridin' fer cattle the most of my
  life.
I ain't got no family, I ain't got no wife,
I ain't got no kith, I ain't got no kin,
I allus will finish what ere I begin.
I rode down in Texas where the cow-
  boys are tall,
The State's pretty big but the hosses
  er small.
Fer singin' to cattle, I'm hard to outdo;
I'm a high-lopin cowboy, an' a wild
  buckeroo.

I rode in Montana an' in Idaho;
I rode for Terasus in old Mexico.
I rope mountain lion an' grizzly bear,
I use cholla cactus fer combin' my hair.
I cross the dry desert, no water be-
  tween,
I rode through Death Valley without
  no canteen.
At ridin' dry deserts I'm hard to outdo;
I'm a high-lopin cowboy an' a wild
  buckeroo.

Why, I kin talk Spanish and Injun to
    boot,
I pack me a knife and a pistol to shoot.
I got no Senorita, an' I got no squaw,
I got no sweetheart, ner mother-in-law.
I never been tied to no apron strings,
I ain't no devil, but I got no wings.
At uh dodgin' the ladies, I'm hard to
    outdo;
I'm a high-lopin' cowboy, an' a wild
    buckeroo.

I drink red whiskey, an' I don't like
    beer,
I don't like mutton, but I do like steer.
I will let you alone if you leave me be,
But don't you get tough an' crawl on
    me.
I'll fight you now at the drop of a hat,
You'll think you're sacked up with a
    scratchin' wild cat.
At rough ready mixin' I'm hard to
    outdo;
I'm a high-lopin' cowboy, an' a wild
    buckeroo.

THE VALLEY OF LISTLESS DREAMS

When the autumn of life is over,
And the winter of life just begun,
We unfold the leaves of life's pages
And in retrospect read them, each one.
When we've tasted the sweet and the
    bitter
While sailing life's turbulent streams,
Then we drift to the still serene waters
Of the Valley of Listless Dreams.

As life's golden sunset is nearing,
When youth has surrendered at last;
As the clouds of the future are clearing,
And they blend in the haze of the past;
When time has called us to vespers,
And we hearken to nature's themes,
Our ears are attuned to the whispers
Of the Valley of Listless Dreams.

No fear of the here or hereafter,
Nor suspense at the nearing of death;
Enough for today, today's laughter,
Sufficient today, today's breath.
Ah! yes, 'tis age with its insight
That is barren of youth's selfish schemes,
And 'tis age that basks in the twlight
Of the Valley of Listless Dreams.

When we see the fine demarcation
That lies twixt the living and dead,
As our tired eyes gaze with indifference
At the rotting of life's silken thread.
When life's golden youth has departed
In the limbo of past, then it seems
That we cherish the hours we spend here
In the Valley of Listless Dreams.

When the autumn of life is over
And the winter of life just begun,
We unfold the leaves of life's pages
And in retrospect read them, each
    one.

MEDITATION

The soft wind sways the whispering
    grass,
The sun sinks low o'er the Western
    pass;
As a coyote mingles his dismal howl,
With the sad, sweet notes of a lone
    hoot owl.

A hawk soars lazily up on high,
A speck of black in a crimson sky,
As a nightingale croons his evening song,
A grey wolf slinks through the shadows
    long.

The shadows deepen; then the rising
    moon,
With its silvery radiance all too
    soon
Dispels the darkness and brings to
    view
The myriad things of the night anew.

A chuckling porcupine wends his way
To his feeding ground, 'ere the break of day;
A mighty stag comes browsing on,
With a graceful doe and a timid fawn.

Then a sadness grips you like a pall
In the silvery gloom where the sha-
dows fall;
Then you wonder why you feel de-
pressed;
Though you are alone, you have not
guessed.
'Tis because you are a poacher there,
Unclean, where nature's breast lies
bare,
And you would this spot so sweet,
so grand,
Might remain untarnished by human
hand.

But e'en this spot shall see the day
When it will fall the easy prey,
Of lust and greed, and in the place
Where yon pine sways in supple grace
An axe-scarred stump will stand, in-
stead,
Bowing in shame its branchless head,
And down the rivers will float the
spoils,
All helpless victims to human toils.

The drumming grouse will seek in vain
For the cozy coverts to nest again.
The quaking aspens will tremble ashamed
For the towering forests so torn and maimed.
The work of aeons will fall away
To the reaper's stroke in a single day,
Though the future ages may never mend
The scars of greed till the end of end.

WHEN DESERT FLOWERS BLOOM

by Curley Fletcher

When the flow'rs of the des-ert are bloom - ing And the swal - low is build ing its nest ___ Where the Guar - di - an Peaks are a - loom - ing O'er my old des - ert home in the West; ___

Published in Standard Folio Size